AA

# FRENCH
## Phrasebook for Kids

# About this book

Jane Wightwick
had the idea

Wina Gunn
wrote the pages

Leila & Zeinah Gaafar
(aged 10 and 12) drew
the first pictures in
each chapter

Robert Bowers
(aged 52) drew the other
pictures, and designed
the book

Marie-Claude Dunleavy did the
French stuff (with some help
from Alix Fontaine)

Important things
that must be included

© g-and-w publishing 2019

All rights reserved. This publication or any part of it may
not be copied or reproduced by any means without the
prior permission of the publisher. All enquiries should
be directed to the publisher.

A CIP catalogue record for this book is available from
the British Library

ISBN 978-0-7495-8367-5

Published by AA Publishing (a trading name of
AA Media Limited, whose registered office is
Grove House, Lutyens Close, Basingstoke, Hampshire
RG24 8AG. Registered number 06112600).

Printed and bound in China by
1010 Printing International Limited

A05864

# What's inside

## Making friends

How to be cool with the group

## Wanna play?

Our guide to joining in everything from hide-and-seek to the latest electronic game

## Feeling hungry

Order your favourite foods or go local

## Looking good

Make sure you keep up with all those essential fashions

## Hanging out

At the pool, beach, or theme park - don't miss out on the action

## Pocket money

Spend it here!

## Grown-up talk

If you really, really have to!

## Extra stuff

All the handy things - numbers, months, time, days of the week

dad
papa
👄 pah-pah

grandpa
papi
👄 pah-pee

my big brother
mon grand frère
👄 mo gro frair

grandma
mamie
👄 ma-mee

mum
maman
👄 ma-mon

my little sister
ma petite sœur
👄 ma pteet sir

MAKING FRIENDS

## Half a step this way

stepfather/stepmother
beau-père/belle-mère
🫦 bow pair/bel mair

stepbrother/stepsister
beau-frère/belle-sœur
🫦 bow frair/bel sir

half brother/half sister
demi frère/demi sœur
🫦 dumee frair/dumee sir

Hi!
Salut!
🫦 saloo

What's your name?
Comment tu t'appelles?
🫦 ko-mo too tapel

My name's ...
Je m'appelle ...
🫦 juh mapel

Kissing is extremely popular among French children. You can't possibly say hello to your friends in the morning without kissing them on both cheeks.

Try this in front of your mirror if your friends at home won't let you experiment on them.

**from Canada**
du Canada
👄 doo kana-da

**from Ireland**
d'Irlande
👄 deer-lond

**from Wales**
du Pays de Galles
👄 doo pay-ee duh gal

**from Scotland**
d'Écosse
👄 day-cos

**from the United States**
des États-Unis
👄 days etaz-oo-nee

**from England**
d'Angleterre
👄 donglutair

10

# Texting

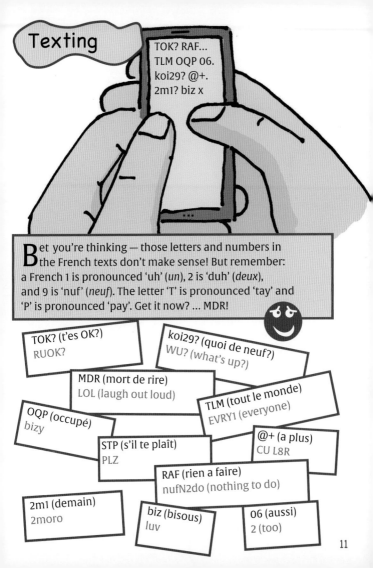

TOK? RAF...
TLM OQP 06.
koi29? @+.
2m1? biz x

Bet you're thinking — those letters and numbers in the French texts don't make sense! But remember: a French 1 is pronounced 'uh' (*un*), 2 is 'duh' (*deux*), and 9 is 'nuf' (*neuf*). The letter 'T' is pronounced 'tay' and 'P' is pronounced 'pay'. Get it now? ... MDR!

TOK? (t'es OK?)
RUOK?

koi29? (quoi de neuf?)
WU? (what's up?)

MDR (mort de rire)
LOL (laugh out loud)

TLM (tout le monde)
EVRY1 (everyone)

OQP (occupé)
bizy

STP (s'il te plaît)
PLZ

@+ (a plus)
CU L8R

RAF (rien a faire)
nufN2do (nothing to do)

2m1 (demain)
2moro

biz (bisous)
luv

06 (aussi)
2 (too)

How old are you?
T'as quel âge?
👄 ta kel azh

12 years old
Douze ans
👄 dooz on

Happy birthday!
Bon anniversaire!
👄 bon anee-versair

What's your star sign?
C'est quoi, ton signe astrologique?
👄 say kwa toh seen-yastrolojeek

When's your birthday?
C'est quand, ton anniversaire?
👄 say kon, ton anee-versair

# Star signs

### AQUARIUS
Jan. 21 – Feb. 19
le Verseau 🗣 luhver-so

### PISCES
Feb. 20 – Mar. 20
les Poissons 🗣 lay pwason-so

### ARIES
Mar. 21 – Apr. 20
le Bélier 🗣 luh belly-er

### TAURUS
Apr. 21 – May. 21
le Taureau 🗣 luh tor-oh

### GEMINI
May 22 – June 21
les Gémeaux 🗣 lay jem-oh

### CANCER
June 22 – July 23
le Cancer 🗣 luh cancer

### LEO
July 24 – Aug. 23
le Lion 🗣 luh lee-on

### VIRGO
Aug. 24 – Sep. 23
la Vierge 🗣 la vee-erj

### LIBRA
Sep. 24 – Oct. 23
la Balance 🗣 la ba-lons

### SCORPIO
Oct. 24 – Nov. 22
le Scorpion 🗣 luh scorpion

### SAGITTARIUS
Nov. 23 – Dec. 21
le Sagittaire 🗣 luh sajitair

### CAPRICORN
Dec. 22 – Jan. 20
le Capricorne 🗣 luh capricorn

13

14

football le foot
🗣 luh foot

rollerblading
le roller
🗣 luh roller

music
la musique
🗣 la mew-zeek

electronic games
les jeux électroniques
🗣 lay juh ay-lek-tro-neek

tv
la télé
🗣 la taylay

comics
la BD
🗣 la bay-day

teddy bears
les nounours
🗣 lay noonoor

school l'école
🗣 lay-kol

spiders les araignées
🗣 layz aran-nyay

15

What's your favourite ...?
Quel est ton/ta ... préféré(e)?

🗣 kel ay ton/tah ... preh-fairay

group
(ton) groupe
🗣 (ton) groop

colour
(ta) couleur
🗣 (tah) koo-luh

Page 69

game
(ton) jeu
🗣 (ton) juh

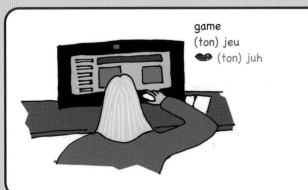

**snack**
(ton) goûter
🫦 (ton) gootay

**ringtone**
(ta) sonnerie
🫦 (tah) soneree

**animal**
(ton) animal
🫦 (ton) a-nee-mal

**team**
(ton) équipe
🫦 (ton) ekeep

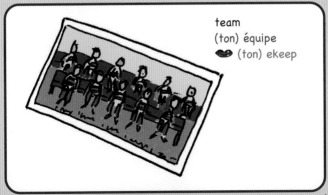

17

# Talk about your pets

He's hungry
Il a faim
👄 eel ah fam

She's sleeping
Elle fait dodo
👄 el fay dodo

Can I stroke your dog?
Je peux caresser ton chien?
👄 juh puh karessay
ton shyan

Do you have
any pets?
T'as des animaux de
compagnie?
👄 tah dayz
animoh duh
kopanyee

18

**dog**
le chien
🗣 luh shee-an

**cat**
le chat
🗣 luh sha

**guinea pig**
le cochon d'Inde
🗣 luh ko-shon d'and

**snake**
le serpent
🗣 luh sir-pon

**hamster**
le hamster
🗣 luh amster

**parakeet**
la perruche
🗣 la peroosh

### My Little doggy goes oua-oua-oua!

A French doggy (that's "toutou" in baby language) doesn't say "woof, woof", it says "oua, oua" (*waa-waa*). A French sheep says "bêê, bêê" (*bear-bear*) and a cluck-cluck in French chicken-speak is "cot-cot" (*ko-ko*). But cats do say "miaow" whether they're speaking French or English!

# Talk about school (if you can stand it)

geography
la géo
🗣 la jay-o

PE
la gym
🗣 la jeem

art
le dessin
🗣 luh dessa

French
le français
🗣 luh fron-say

maths
les maths
🗣 lay mat

English
l'anglais
🗣 lon-glay

music
la musique
🗣 la mew-zeek

history
l'histoire
🗣 lis-twar

science
les sciences
🗣 lay see-yons

l'informatique

lanfor-mateek

## Way unfair!

French children have very long vacation breaks: 9 weeks in the summer and another 6–7 weeks throughout the rest of the year. But before you turn green with envy, you might not like the mounds of *"devoirs de vacances"* (*duh-vwa duh vacans*), that's "vacation homework"! And if you fail your exams, the teachers could make you repeat the whole year with your little sister!

# Talk about your phone

That's ancient
Il est super vieux!
🗨 eel ay super vyuh

I've run
out of credit
J'ai plus de
forfait
🗨 jay ploo
duh forfay

What's your mobile like?
Il est comment ton
portable?
🗨 eel ay komon ton
portabluh

Lucky!
Trop de chance!
🗨 troh duh shons

What a cool ringtone!
Elle est géniale ta sonnerie!
🗨 el ay jenyal ta soneree

# Gossip

Can you keep a secret?
Tu peux garder
un secret?
🗣 too puh
garday
uh sekray

Do you have a boyfriend
(a girlfriend)?
T'as un petit ami
(une petite amie)?
🗣 tah uh
pteet amee
(oon pteet
amee)

An OK guy/An OK girl
Un mec sympa/
Une fille sympa
🗣 uh mek sampa/
oon fee sampa

What a bossy-boots!
Quel commandant!
🗣 kel comon-don

He/She's nutty!
Il/Elle est dingue!
🗣 eel/el ay dang

What a misery guts!
Quel râleur!
🗣 kel rah-luh

# You won't make many friends saying this!

**Bog off!**
*Dégage!*
🗣 day-gaj

**Shut up!**
*La ferme!*
🗣 la ferm

If you're fed up with someone, and you want to say something like "you silly ...!" or "you stupid ...!", you can start with "*espèce de*" (which actually means "piece of ...") and add anything you like. What about ...

**Stupid banana!**
*Espèce de banane!*
(espes duh banan)

or ...

**Silly sausage!**
*Espèce d'andouille!*
(espes don-dooy)

Take your pick. It should do the trick. You could also try "*espèce d'idiot!*" (*espes dee-dyo*). You don't need a translation here, do you?

# You might have to say

Bother!
La vache!
🗣 la vash
That means "Cow"!

Rats!
Zut!
🗣 zoot

"Did someone call me?"

That's not funny
C'est pas marrant
🗣 say pah marron

That's plenty!
C'est bon!
🗣 say bon

I'm fed up
J'en ai ras-le-bol
🗣 jon nay ral-bol

Stop!
Arrête!
🗣 aret

I want to go home!
Je veux rentrer chez moi!
🗣 juh vuh rentray
shay mwah

I don't care
Je m'en fiche
🗣 juh mon feesh

At last!
C'est pas trop tôt!
🗣 say pah tro toe

27

# Saying goodbye

**Here's my address**
Voilà mon adresse
💋 vla mon adres

**What's your address?**
Tu m'donnes ton adresse?
💋 too mdon ton adres

**Come to visit me**
Viens chez moi
💋 vya shay mwa

H ow do you say goodbye
to a skeleton?

*Bone Voyage!*

Have a good trip!
Bon voyage!
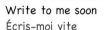 bon vwoy-arj

Write to me soon
Écris-moi vite
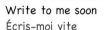 ekree mwa veet

Send me a text
Envois-moi un texto
 onvwa-mwa uh texto

Let's chat online
On chat sur internet
 on "chat" syur internet

Bye!
Au revoir!
 oh rev-wa

What's your email address?
C'est quoi ton e-mail?
 say kwa ton e-mail

*⊃□*@3◇*@㕲.com

# WANNA PLAY?

skipping rope
l'élastique
 lelasteek

table tennis
le ping-pong
luh "ping pong"

**MP3 player**
le baladeur
👄 luh balad-er

**yo-yo**
le yo-yo
👄 luh yo-yo

**mobile phone**
le portable
👄 luh porta-bluh

WANNA PLAY?

Do you want to play ...?
Tu veux jouer ...?
🗨 too vuh joo-ay

... table football?
... au baby-foot?
🗨 oh baby foot

... cards?
... aux cartes?
🗨 oh kart

... on the computer?
... sur l'ordinateur?
🗨 syur lordee-nater

... noughts and crosses?
... au morpion?
🗨 oh more-pyon

33

# Care for a game of cat or leap sheep?!

I n France, playing tag is called playing "at cat", *à chat* (*asha*). Whoever is "it" is the cat, *le chat* (*luh sha*). And you don't play "leap frog", you play "leap sheep": *saute mouton* (*sote moo-ton*). Have you ever seen a sheep leaping?

**Can my friend play too?**
Mon copain peut jouer aussi?
🗣 mo kopan puh jooway oh-see

**I have to ask my parents**
Il faut que je demande à mes vieux
🗣 eel foh kuh juh daymon ah may vyuh

# Make yourself heard

# Who dares?

**You're it!**
Touché!
 tooshay

**Race you!**
On fait la course?
on fay la koors?

**I'm first**
C'est moi le premier
say mwa luh pre-myay

**Who's winning?**
Qui c'est qui gagne?
🗣 kee say kee gan-yuh

**Ready, steady, go!**
A vos marques, prêts, partez!
🗣 ah voh mark, preh, partay

**Where's the finish?**
Où est la ligne d'arrivée?
🗣 oo ay la leen-yuh
dareevay

**I need a head start**
J'ai besoin de prendre de l'avance
🗣 jay buzwa duh prondruh duh la-vons

37

# Electronic games

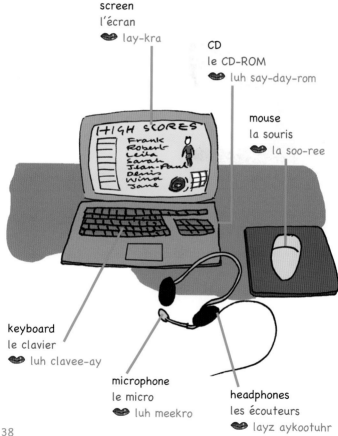

**screen**
l'écran
🗣 lay-kra

**CD**
le CD-ROM
🗣 luh say-day-rom

**mouse**
la souris
🗣 la soo-ree

**keyboard**
le clavier
🗣 luh clavee-ay

**microphone**
le micro
🗣 luh meekro

**headphones**
les écouteurs
🗣 layz aykootuhr

38

Show me
Montre-moi
 montruh mwa

What do I do?
Qu'est-ce que je fais?
😛 keskuh juh fay

Am I dead?
Ch'suis mort?
😛 shwee more

Shoot-em-up!
Tue-les!
😛 tew-lay

How many lives do I have?
J'ai combien de vies?
😛 jay konbee-yah duh vee

How many levels are there?
Y'a combien de niveaux?
😛 yah konbee-yah de neevo

# It's virtual fun!

Do you have WiFi?
T'as le WiFi?
🐛 ta luh weefee

Send me a message.
Envois-moi un message.

How do i join?
Comment je m'inscris?

I'm not old enough.
Je suis pas assez grand.

I'm not allowed.
J'ai pas le droit.

I don't know who you are.
Je sais pas qui vous êtes.

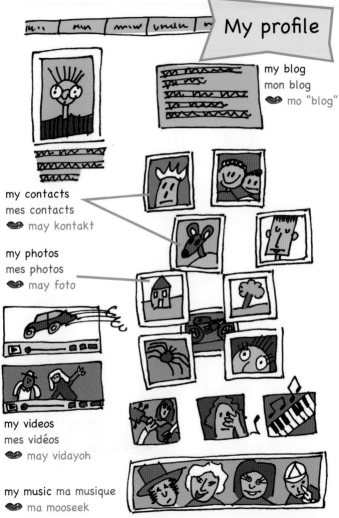

my blog
mon blog
🗨 mo "blog"

my contacts
mes contacts
🗨 may kontakt

my photos
mes photos
🗨 may foto

my videos
mes vidéos
🗨 may vidayoh

my music ma musique
🗨 ma mooseek

41

# Non couch-potato activities!

tennis
le tennis
🗣 luh "tennis"

trampolining
le trampoline
🗣 luh "trampoline"

bowling
le bowling
🗣 luh "bowling"

swimming
la natation
🗣 la natasee-on

42

hockey
le hockey
👄 luh okee

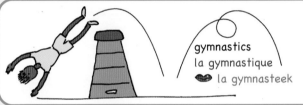

gymnastics
la gymnastique
👄 la gymnasteek

ballet
le ballet
👄 luh ballay

basketball
le basket
👄 luh basket

and, of course, we haven't forgotten "*le foot*"...

# football

**boots**
les godasses
 lay godas

**football strip**
les affaires de foot
lay affaires de foot
layz afayr duh foot

**ref**
l'arbitre
lar-beetruh

**shin pads**
les protèges-tibias
lay protej-tibya

**Well played!**
Bien joué
beeyah joo-way

44

**Pass! Passe!**
pas

**Offside!**
Hors-jeu!
🗣 or-juh

**Hands!**
Y'a eu mains!
🗣 Ya ew man

**You're on my team**
T'es dans mon équipe
🗣 tay don mon ay-keep

**crossbar**
la barre
🗣 la bar

**goalpost**
le poteau
🗣 luh potto

**goal**
le but
🗣 luh boo

**goalie**
le gardien
🗣 luh gardyen

45

defender
le défenseur
🗣 luh dayfonsur

attacker
l'attaquant
🗣 latakon

Foul!
Coup-franc!
🗣 koo fron

Penalty!
Le penalty!
🗣 luh paynalty

He pushed me!
Il m'a poussé!
🗣 eel ma poo-say

Goal!
Goal!
🗣 just say it!

46

# Keeping the others in line

Not like that!
Pas comme ça!
🗣 pah kom sa

You cheat! Tricheur! (boys only)
Tricheuse! (girls only)
🗣 tree-sher/tree-sherz

I'm not playing anymore
Je joue plus
🗣 juh joo ploo

It's not fair!
C'est pas juste!
🗣 say pah joost

Stop it!
Arrête!
🗣 aret

# Showing off

a handstand?
le poirier?
🗨 luh pwa-riyay

Can you do ...
Tu sais faire ...
🗨 too say fair

Look at me!
Regarde-moi!
🗨 re-gard mwa

a cartwheel?
la roue?
🗨 la roo

this?
ça?
🗨 sa

48

## Impress your French friends with this!

You can show off to your new French friends by practising this tongue twister:

*Si ces six sausissons-ci sont six sous, ces six sausissons-ci sont très chers*
*see say see soseeson see son see soo, say see*
*soseeson see son tray shair*

(This means "If these six sausages cost six sous, these six sausages are very expensive.")

Then see if they can do as well with this English one:

"She sells seashells on the seashore,
but the shells she sells aren't seashells, I'm sure."

# For a rainy day

pack of cards
un jeu de cartes
🗨 uh juh duh kart

my deal/your deal
à moi la donne/à toi la donne
🗨 a mwa la don/a twa la don

king
le roi
🗨 luh rwa

queen
la dame
🗨 la dam

jack
le valet
🗨 luh valay

joker
le joker
🗨 luh jokair

trèfle
🗨 tray-fluh

cœur
🗨 kur

pique
🗨 peek

carreau
🗨 karo

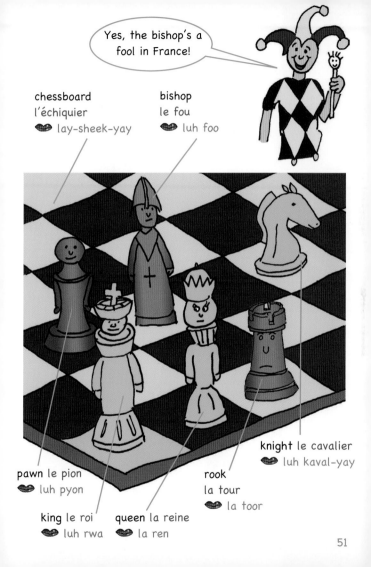

51

# Grub (la bouffe)

**I'm starving**
J'ai une faim de loup
 jay oon fam duh loo

That means "I have the hunger of a wolf"!

*le loup*

**Please can I have ...**
Donnez-moi, s'il vous plaît ...
donay mwa, seel voo play

... a chocolate pastry
un pain au chocolat
👄 uh pan oh shokolah

... a croissant
un croissant
👄 uh kruh-son

... an apple turnover
un chausson aux pommes
👄 uh show-son oh pom

... a chocolate eclair
un éclair au chocolat
👄 uh eklair oh shokolah

... a bun with raisins
un pain aux raisins
👄 uh pan oh rayzan

## Food noises

Chocolate eclair? "*Miam, miam!*"
Snail pancake? "*Beurk!*" If you're
going to make food noises, you'll

need to know how
to do it properly
in French! "Yum,
yum!" is out in French. You should say
"*Miam, miam!*" And "Yuk!" is "*Beurk*"
(pronounced "burk"), but be careful
not to let adults hear you say this!

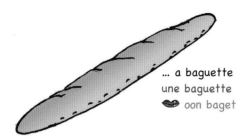

... a baguette
une baguette
🗣 oon baget

... a pancake
une crêpe
🗣 oon krep

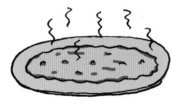

... a waffle
une gaufre
🗣 oon go-fruh

## Did you know?

A lot of children have hot chocolate for breakfast in the morning and some of them will dip their bread or croissants in it. It gets very soggy and Mum is sure not to like this!

## Drink up

I'm dying for a drink
Je meurs de soif
👄 juh mur duh swaf

I'd like ...
Je voudrais ...
👄 juh voodray

... a coke
... un coca
👄 uh koka

... an orange juice
... un jus d'orange
👄 uh joo doronj

... an apple juice
... un jus de pommes
👄 uh joo duh pom

... a lemonade
... une limonade
 oon leemonad

You can also have your lemonade with flavoured syrup –then it's called "*diabolo.*" The most well-known is "*diabolo menthe*", lemonade with mint syrup – hmmm!

... a syrup
un sirop
 uh seero

... a milkshake
... un milkshake
 uh meelkshek

You get your hot chocolate in a bowl (and that, at least, is a decent amount).

... a hot chocolate
... un chocolat
 uh shokolah

# How did you like it?

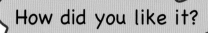

That's lovely
C'est super-bon
 say soopair-bon

That's yummy
C'est géant
 say jay-on

I don't like that
J'aime pas ça
 jem pah sa

I'm stuffed
J'ai trop bouffé
 jay tro boofay

I can't eat that
Je mange pas ça
 juh monj pah sa

That's gross
C'est dégoûtant
 say day-gooton

# A "crunchy man" sandwich, please

You never thought you could crunch up a man in France and get away with it, did you? Well, in France a grilled ham-and-cheese sandwich is:

un croque-monsieur
🗨 uh krok murs-yur

... that means a "crunchy man". There's also a "crunchy woman"!

un croque-madame
🗨 uh krok ma-dam

... which is the same but with a fried egg on top.

## Tails of snails

Did you know that snails have to be put in a bucket of salt water for three days to clean out their insides (don't ask!). After that they are baked in the oven in their shells and eaten with tons of garlic butter. And many French kids still love them!

Parties

French children often sing "Happy Birthday" in English when the candles are blown out on the cake. So you can practise singing the words with a French accent!

**balloon** la balle
🗣 la bal

appee birzday too yoo!
appee birzday too yoo!

Can I have some more?
Je peux en avoir d'autre?
🗣 juh puh avwah door-truh

**party hat**
le chapeau cotillon
🗣 luh shapoh koteeyon

This is for you
C'est pour toi
🗣 say poor twa

61

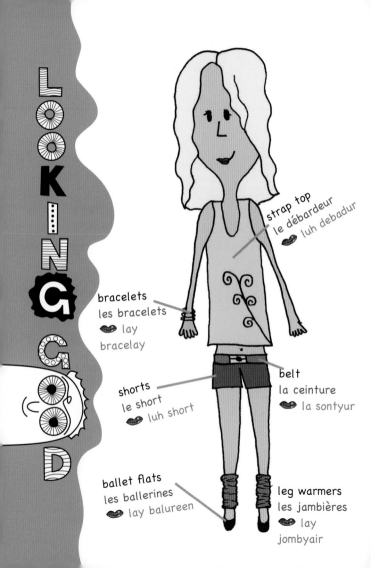

LOOKING GOOD

strap top
le débardeur
💋 luh debadur

bracelets
les bracelets
💋 lay
bracelay

belt
la ceinture
💋 la sontyur

shorts
le short
💋 luh short

ballet flats
les ballerines
💋 lay balureen

leg warmers
les jambières
💋 lay
jombyair

cap
la casquette
🗨 la kasket

earphones
les écouteurs
🗨 lays eh-
koo ter

hoodie
la cagoule
🗨 la kagool

jeans
le jean
🗨 luh jeen

trainers
les baskets
🗨 lay basket

LOOKING GOOD

# Clothes

sweatshirt
le sweat
🗣 luh swet

jeans
le jean
🗣 luh "jean"

T-shirt
le T-shirt
🗣 luh "T-shirt"

football shirt
le maillot de foot
🗣 luh mayo duh foot

trainers
les baskets
🗣 lay basket

shoes
les chaussures
🗣 lay show-soor

64

dress
la robe
🗣 la rob

skirt
la jupe
🗣 la joop

trousers
le pantalon
🗣 luh panta-lon

## Where's my trouser?!

The French don't wear "trousers" or "jeans" – they wear only one of them: un pantalon (*uh pantaloh*); un jean (*uh jeen*). Strange, could've sworn they had two legs!

That T-shirt, please
Ce T-shirt-là, s'il vous plaît
suh "T-shirt" là, seel voo play

Cool tattoo!
Tatouage cool!
tattoo-arj cool

The pink frilly one
Le rose à frous-frous
luh roz a froo froo

The purple
stripey one
Le violet à rayures
luh vee-oh-lay
a rayure

Awesome
miniskirt!
Minijupe d'enfer!
minee-joop donfair

Where's my
skateboard?
Où est mon skate-board?
oo ay mon "skateboard"?

spotty
à pois
🗨 a pwa

flowery
à fleurs
🗨 a fler

frilly
à frous-frous
🗨 a froo froo

glittery
à paillettes
🗨 a pie-et

stripey
à rayures
🗨 a rayure

67

# Make it up!

lip gloss
le gloss
💋 luh gloss

nail varnish
le vernis à ongles
💋 luh vairnee
a ongluh

glitter gel
le gel à paillettes
💋 luh jel a pie-yet

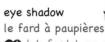

earrings
les boucles d'oreilles
💋 lay boo-kluh doray

I need a mirror
J'ai besoin
d'un miroir
💋 jay buzwa
duh mirwa

eye shadow
le fard à paupières
💋 luh fardah po-pyair

Can you lend
me your
straighteners?
Tu peux me prêter
ton fer à lisser?
💋 too puh muh
pretay ton fair
a leezay

68

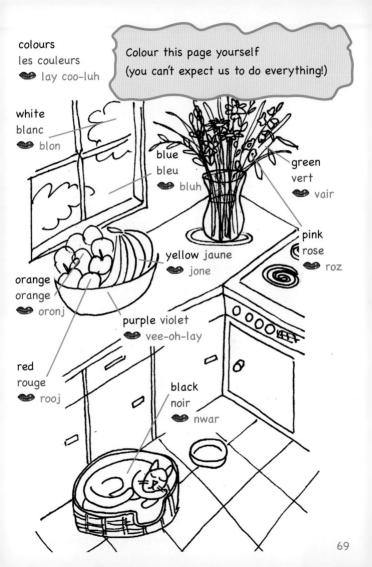

colours
les couleurs
🗣 lay coo-luh

Colour this page yourself
(you can't expect us to do everything!)

white
blanc
🗣 blon

blue
bleu
🗣 bluh

green
vert
🗣 vair

pink
rose
🗣 roz

yellow jaune
🗣 jone

orange
orange
🗣 oronj

purple violet
🗣 vee-oh-lay

red
rouge
🗣 rooj

black
noir
🗣 nwar

69

What should we do?
Qu'est-ce qu'on fait?
👄 kesk on fay

Can I come?
Je peux venir?
👄 juh puh vuneer

Where do you all hang out?
Où traînez-vous?
👄 oo trainay voo

That's mega!
C'est géant!
👄 say jay-on

I'm (not) allowed
J'ai (pas) le droit
👄 jay (pa) luh drwa

**Let's go back** On y retourne
🗣 onny rutoorn

**That gives me goose bumps (or "chicken flesh" in French!)**
Ça m'donne la chair de poule
🗣 sa mdon la shair duh pool

**I'm bored to death**
C'est mortel
🗣 say mortell

**That's funny**
C'est marrant
🗣 say maron

73

# Beach babes

Can I borrow this?
Tu me prêtes ça?
🗨 too muh pret sa

Let's hit the beach
On va à la plage
🗨 on va a la plarj

Is this your bucket?
C'est ton seau?
🗨 say toh so

You can bury me
Tu peux m'enterrer
🗨 too puh moterray

Stop throwing sand!
Arrête de jeter du sable!
🗨 arret duh jetay
dew sabluh

Watch out for my eyes!
Attention à mes yeux!
🗨 attensee-on
a maiz yuh

74

sea
la mer
🐌 la mair

beach
la plage
🐌 la plarj

snorkel
le tuba
🐌 luh tew-ba

towel
la serviette
🐌 la sir-vee-et

bathing costume
le maillot
🐌 luh my-yo

bucket
le seau
🐌 luh so

spade la pelle
🐌 la pel

sandcastle
le château de sable
🐌 luh shato
duh sabluh

shells
les coquillages
🐌 lay kokeeyarj

## How to get rid of your parents and eat lots of chocolate!

In France there are great beach clubs that organise all sorts of games as well as competitions (sandcastles, sports, etc.). The prizes are often given by large companies who make kids' stuff such as chocolate and toys. Insist on signing up!

# It's going swimmingly!

*How to make a splash in French!*

Let's hit the swimming pool
On va à la piscine
🗣 on va a la piseen

Can you swim (underwater)?
Tu sais nager (sous l'eau)?
🗣 too say najay (soo lo)

Me too/I can't
Moi aussi/Moi pas
🗣 mwa os-see/ mwa pa

Can you dive?
Tu sais plonger?
🗣 too say plonjay

I'm getting changed
Je me change 🗣 juh muh shanj

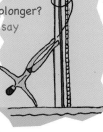

76

**Can you do ...?**
Tu sais faire ...?
🗣 too say fair

**backstroke**
le dos crawlé
🗣 luh doe krolay

**butterfly**
le papillon
🗣 luh papeeyon

**crawl**
le crawl
🗣 luh krol

**breaststroke**
la brasse 🗣 la brass

**slide**
le toboggan
🗣 luh tobogan

**goggles**
les lunettes de plongée
🗣 lay loonet duh plonjay

# Downtown

Do you know the way?
Tu connais le chemin?
👄 too konay luh shema

## Pooper-scoopers on wheels!

You might see bright green-and-white motorcycles with funny vacuum cleaners on the side riding around town scooping up the dog poop. The people riding the bikes look like astronauts! (Well, you'd want protection too, wouldn't you?)

Let's ask
On va demander
👄 o va demonday

bus
le bus
👄 luh boos

**Is it far?**
C'est loin?
🗣 say lwan

**Are we allowed in here?**
On a le droit d'entrer ici?
🗣 on a luh drwa dentray eessee

car
la bagnole
🗣 la banyol

The "proper" French word for car is "*voiture*" (*vwat-yure*), but you'll look very uncool saying this. Stick to "*bagnole*" (*banyol*), or if the car is a wreck, try "*tacot*" (*taco*) for even more street cred: "*Quel tacot!*" (*kel tako*—"What an old banger!*").

79

# Park yourself here

swings la balançoire
🗣 la balonswar

climbing frame
la cage à poules
🗣 la kaj ah pool

playground l'aire de jeu
🗣 lair duh juh

grass l'herbe
🗣 lairb

tree l'arbre
🗣 larbruh

slide
le toboggan
🗣 luh tobogan

park le parc 🗣 luh park

Can we play ball games?
On peut jouer au ballon?
🗣 on puh jooway oh balon

roundabout
le tourniquet 🗣 luh toornikay

sandpit
le bac à sable
🗣 luh bakah sabluh

Can I have a go? Je peux
essayer? 🗣 juh puh esay-yay

# Picnic (le pique-nique)

I hate wasps
Je déteste les guêpes
🗣 juh daytest
lay gep

Move over!
Pousse-toi!
🗣 poos twa

bread
le pain 🗣 luh pan

Let's sit here
On s'assoie ici?
🗣 on saswa eessee

napkin
la serviette
🗣 la sir-vee-et

ham le jambon
🗣 luh jambon

cheese
le fromage
🗣 luh fromarj

yoghurt
le yaourt
🗣 luh ya-oort

crisps
les chips
🗣 lay sheep

**drinks**
les boissons
 lay bwason

**knife**
le couteau
 luh koo-toe

**spoon**
la cuillère
la kwee-yeah

**fork**
la fourchette
la four-shet

**bees**
les abeilles
layz abay

**wasps**
les guêpes
 lay gep

**ants**
les fourmis
lay foor-mee

83

# Wake up, campers!

tent la tente
🗣 la tont

tent peg
le piquet de tente
🗣 luh peekay duh tont

camper van
le camping-car
🗣 luh komping car

penknife
le couteau suisse
🗣 luh kootoh swees

camping stove
le camping gaz
🗣 luh komping gaz

sleeping bag le sac de couchage
🗣 luh sak duh kooshaj

torch
la lampe de poche
🗣 la lomp
duh posh

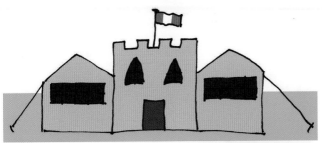

That tent's a palace!
Cette tente, c'est la classe!
🗣 set tont, say la klas

campfire
le feu de camp
🗣 luh fuh duh komp

I've lost my torch
J'ai paumé ma lampe de poche
🗣 jay pomay ma lomp duh posh

These showers are gross!
Ces douches sont crades!
🗣 say doosh son krad

Where does the rubbish go?
Où est-ce qu'on jette les ordures?
🗣 oo eskon jet layz ordyur

# All the fun of the fair

**helter-skelter**
le toboggan
🗣 luh tobogan

**big wheel**
la grande roue
🗣 la grond roo

**house of mirrors**
le palais des glaces
🗣 luh palay day glas

**Let's try this**
On essaie ça?
🗣 on essay sa

**bumper cars**
les autos
tamponneuses
🗣 layz oto
tomponerz

**roundabout**
le manège
🗨 luh manayj

**It's (too) fast**
Ça va (trop) vite
🗨 sa va (tro) veet

**That's for babies**
C'est pour les petits
🗨 say poor lay ptee

**Do you get wet in here?**
On sort mouillé d'ici?
🗨 on sor moo-yay deessee

**I'm not going on my own**
J'y vais pas tout seul
🗨 jee vay pa too surl

87

## Disco nights

**mirror ball**
la boule multi-facettes
💬 la bool multee-faset

**loudspeakers**
les enceintes
💬 layz onsent

**Can I request a song?**
Je peux demander qu'on passe une chanson? 💬 juh puh dumonday kon pas oon shonso

**The music is really lame**
La musique est vraiment nulle
💬 la mooseek ay vraymon nool

**spotlights**
les spots
💬 lay spot

**DJ**
le DJ
💬 luh "DJ"

**mixing desk** la table de mixage
💬 la tabluh duh meeksarj

**How old do I need to be?**
Quel âge il faut avoir?
🗣 kel aj eel foh avwah

**dance floor**
la piste de danse
🗣 la peest duh dons

**Let's dance!**
On danse!
🗣 on dons

**I love this song!**
J'adore cette chanson!
🗣 jadoor set shonso

89

**POCKET MONEY**

sweets
les bonbons
🗨 lay bonbon

T-shirts
les T-shirts
🗨 lay "T-shirt"

toys
les jouets
🗨 lay joo-ay

shop assistant
le vendeur
🗨 luh von-dur

books

les livres

 lay lee-vruh

les crayons

 lay crayon

Watch out! This means *pencils* NOT crayons!

# What does that sign say?

butcher shop
boucherie
👄 booshree

cake shop
pâtisserie
👄 pateesree

bakery
boulangerie
👄 boolonjree

sweet shop
confiserie
👄 konfeesree

stationary shop
papeterie
👄 paptree

grocer
épicerie
👄 aypeesree

clothes shop
boutique de vêtements
👄 booteek duh vetmon

Do you have some cash?
T'as des sous?
🗣 tah day soo

I'm broke
Je suis fauché
🗣 juh swee foshay

I'm loaded
J'ai plein d'sous
🗣 jay pla dsoo

Here you go
Voilà
🗣 vla

That's a weird shop! Quel magasin bizarre! 🗣 kel maguzah beezar

That's a bargain C'est pas cher
🗣 say pa shair

It's a rip-off
C'est du vol
🗣 say dew vol

93

## Sweet heaven!

**I love this shop**
J'adore cette boutique
🗣 jadore set booteek

**Let's get some sweets**
On va acheter des bonbons
🗣 on va ashtay day bonbon

**Let's get some ice cream**
On va acheter une glace
🗣 on va ashtay oon glas

**lollipops**
des sucettes
🗣 day sooset

**a bar of chocolate**
une tablette de chocolat
🗣 oon tablet duh shokola

**chewing gum**
chewing gum
🗣 just say it, will you!

If you really want to look French and end up with lots of fillings, ask for:

### des Carambars™
(day caram-bar)

*medium-hard toffee-bars, also available in all sorts of fruity flavours; popular for the desperately silly jokes to be found inside the wrappings*

### des Malabars™
(day malabar)

*bubble-gum, also popular for the tattoos provided with them*

### des nounours en chocolat
(day noonoors on shokola)

*teddy-shaped marshmallow-type sweets with a chocolate coating*

### des Mini Berlingot™
(day mini berlingo)

*sugary creamy stuff sold in small squishy packets – a bit like a small version of the "lunchbox" yoghurts*

### des frites
(day freet)

*fruity gums, slightly fizzy, shaped like chips*

### des Dragibus™
(day drajibus)

*multicoloured licorice jelly beans*

# Other things you could buy
(that won't ruin your teeth!)

What are you getting?
Qu'est-ce tu prends?
🗨 keska too pron

That toy, please
Ce jouet là, s'il vous plaît
🗨 suh joo-ay la, seel
voo play

Two postcards, please
Deux cartes postales,
s'il vous plaît
🗨 duh kart
post-tal,
seel voo play

This is rubbish
C'est nul
🗨 say nool

This is cool
C'est cool
🗨 say kool

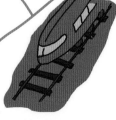

I'm getting ...
J'achète ...
🗣 jashait

... a pen
un stylo
🗣 uh stee-lo

... stamps
des timbres
🗣 day timbruh

... felt-tip pens
des feutres
🗣 day fer-truh

... coloured pencils
des crayons de couleur
🗣 day krayon duh koolur

... a key ring
un porte-clés
🗣 uh port klay

... comics
des BD
🗣 day bay day

... a fridge magnet
un aimant
👄 uh aymon

... a shell box
une boîte à coquillages
👄 oon bwat ah kokeeyaj

... a necklace
un collier
👄 uh kolyay

How much is that?
C'est combien?
👄 say kombee-yah

For many years France's favourite comics have been *Astérix* and *Tintin*. They have both been translated into English, as well as into many other languages. Today children also like to read *Tom Tom et Nana*, *Boule et Bill*, *Natacha* and *Gaston Lagaffe*.

# Money talks

How much pocket money
do you get?
T'as combien d'argent de poche?
🗨 tah komee-yah darjon
duh posh

I only have this much
J'ai seulement ça
🗨 jay sulmo sah

Can you lend me
ten euros?
Tu peux me prêter
dix euros
🗨 too puh muh
pretay dee yooro

No way!
Pas question!
🗨 pa kes-tyo

---

French money is the euro (pronounced *ew-roh*).
A euro is divided into 100 centimes (*senteem*).
Coins:    1, 2, 5, 10, 20, 50 centimes
          1, 2 euros
Notes:    5, 10, 20, 50, 100 euros
Make sure you know how much you are spending before you
blow all your pocket money at once!

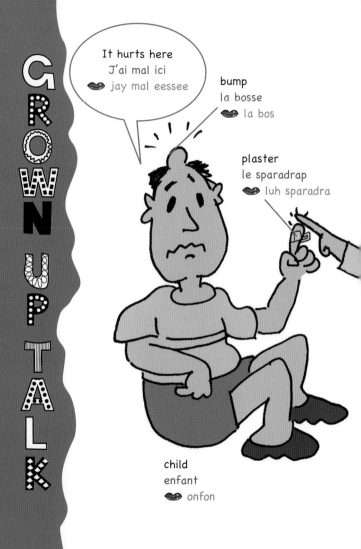

# Help!

Something has dropped/broken
Quelque chose est tombé/cassé
kel-kuh shose ay tombay/kassay

Please
S'il vous plaît
seel voo play

Can you help me?
Vous pouvez m'aider?
voo poovay mayday

Where's the post box?
Où est la boîte aux lettres?
oo ay la bwat oh lettruh

Where are the toilets?
Où sont les toilettes?
oo son lay twalet

102

**I can't manage it**
Je n'y arrive pas
👄 juh nee arreev pah

**Could you pass me that?**
Vous pouvez me passer ça?
👄 voo poovay muh passay sa

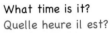

**What time is it?**
Quelle heure il est?
👄 kel ur eelay

**Come and see**
Venez voir
👄 venay vwar

**May I look at your watch?**
Je peux voir sur votre montre?
👄 juh puh vwar syur
votruh montruh

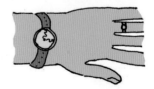

103

# Lost for words

I've lost ...
J'ai perdu ...
🗣 jay perdew

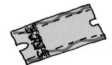

... my ticket
mon billet
🗣 mo beeyay

... my parents
mes parents
🗣 may paron

... my mobile
mon portable
🗣 mo portabluh

... my money mon argent
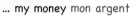 mo arjon

... my shoes
mes chaussures
🗨 may sho-syur

... my sweater
mon pull
🗨 mo pool

... my watch
ma montre
🗨 ma montruh

... my jacket ma veste
🗨 ma vest

## Adults only!

Show this page to adults who can't seem to make themselves clear (it happens).
They will point to a phrase, you read what they mean, and you should all understand each other perfectly.

Ne t'en fais pas
Don't worry

Assieds-toi ici
Sit down here

Quel est ton nom et ton prénom?
What's your name and surname?

Quel âge as-tu?
How old are you?

D'où viens-tu?
**Where are you from?**

Où habites-tu?
**Where are you staying?**

Où est-ce que tu as mal?
**Where does it hurt?**

Est-ce que tu es allergique à quelque chose?
**Are you allergic to anything?**

C'est interdit
**It's forbidden**

Tu dois être accompagné d'un adulte
**You have to have an adult with you**

Je vais chercher quelqu'un qui parle anglais
**I'll get someone who speaks English**

EXTRA STUFF

weather
le temps
🫦 luh toh

numbers les nombres 🫦 lay nombruh

time
l'heure
lur

EXTRA STUFF

# Numbers

There was an English cat called "one, two, three" and a French cat called "un, deux, trois" standing waiting to cross a river. Both were afraid of water, so the English cat suggested that they race across to make it more fun. Who won?

Answer: "One, two, three" because "un, deux, trois" cat sank!

1 un 👄 un

2 deux 👄 duh

3 trois 👄 twa

4 quatre 👄 katruh

5 cinq 👄 sank

6 six 👄 sees

110

7 sept 👄 set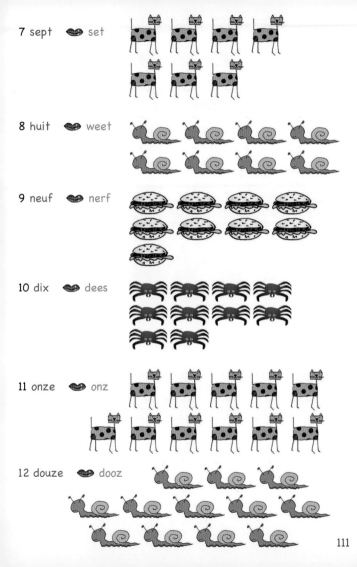

8 huit 👄 weet

9 neuf 👄 nerf

10 dix 👄 dees

11 onze 👄 onz

12 douze 👄 dooz

111

**13** treize 👄 trez

**14** quatorze 👄 catorz

**15** quinze 👄 kanz

| 16 | seize | *sez* | 19 | dix-neuf | *dees-nerf* |
|----|-------|-------|----|----------|-------------|
| 17 | dix-sept | *dees-set* | 20 | vingt | *van* |
| 18 | dix-huit | *dees-weet* | | | |

---

If you want to say "twenty-two", "sixty-five", and so on, you can just put the two numbers together like you do in English:

| 22 | vingt-deux | *van duh* |
|----|------------|-----------|
| 65 | soixante cinq | *swasont sank* |

This works except if you're saying "twenty-one", "sixty-one", and so on. Then you need to add the word for "and" (*et*) in the middle:

| 21 | vingt et un | *vant eh un* |
|----|-------------|--------------|
| 61 | soixante et un | *swasont eh un* |

---

| 30 | trente | *tront* |
|----|--------|---------|
| 40 | quarante | *karont* |
| 50 | cinquante | *sankont* |
| 60 | soixante | *swasont* |
| 70 | soixante-dix | *swasont dees* |
| 80 | quatre-vingts | *katruh van* |
| 90 | quatre-vingt-dix | *katruh van dees* |
| 100 | cent | *sonn* |

a thousand   mille   *meel*

a million   un million   *uh mil-yo*

billions and billions!   des milliards de milliards!
*day meelyar duh meelyar*

The French must be really big on sums! Everything's fine until you reach 70. Instead of saying "seventy," they say "sixty-ten" (*soixante-dix*) and keep counting like this until they reach 80. So 72 is "sixty-twelve" (*soixante douze*), 78 is "sixty-eighteen" (*soixante dix-huit*), and so on.

Just so it doesn't get too easy, for 80 they say "4 twenties"! And to really make your brain ache they continue counting like this until a hundred. So 90 is "4 twenties 10" (*quatre-vingt-dix*), 95 is "4 twenties fifteen" (*quatre-vingt-quinze*) ... you remembered your calculator, didn't you??

# Months

| March | mars | *mars* |
| April | avril | *avreel* |
| May | mai | *meh* |

| June | juin | *joo-wah* |
| July | juillet | *joowee-eh* |
| August | août | *oot* |

| September | septembre | *septombruh* |
| October | octobre | *octobruh* |
| November | novembre | *novombruh* |

| December | décembre | *desombruh* |
| January | janvier | *jonvee-eh* |
| February | février | *fevree-eh* |

Seasons

printemps *prantom*

SPRING

été *eteh*

SUMMER

automne *awtom*

AUTUMN

hiver *eever*

WINTER

118

## Days of the week

| Monday | lundi | *lundee* |
| Tuesday | mardi | *mardee* |
| Wednesday | mercredi | *mecredee* |
| Thursday | jeudi | *jurdee* |
| Friday | vendredi | *vendredee* |
| Saturday | samedi | *samdee* |
| Sunday | dimanche | *deemonsh* |

By the way, French kids don't usually have school on Wednesdays, but they have to go on Saturday mornings. Still, that's half a day less than you!

## Good times

It's ...
Il est ...
👄 eel ay

(one) o'clock
(une) heure
👄 (oon) ur

quarter past (two)
(deux heures) et quart
👄 (duh zur) ay kar

quarter to (four)
(quatre heures) moins le quart
👄 (katr ur) mwan luh kar

half past (three)
(trois heures) et demie
👄 (twa zur) ay demee

**five past (ten)**
(dix heures) cinq
🗣 (dees ur) sank

**twenty past (eleven)**
(onze heures) vingt
🗣 (onz ur) van

**ten to (four)**
(quatre heures) moins dix
🗣 (katr ur) mwan dees

**twenty to (six)**
(six heures) moins vingt
🗣 (sees ur) mwan van

**morning**
matin
🗣 ma-tah

**midday**
midi
🗣 meedee

**afternoon**
après-midi
🗣 apray meedee

**midnight**
minuit
🗣 meenwee

**evening** soir
🗣 swar

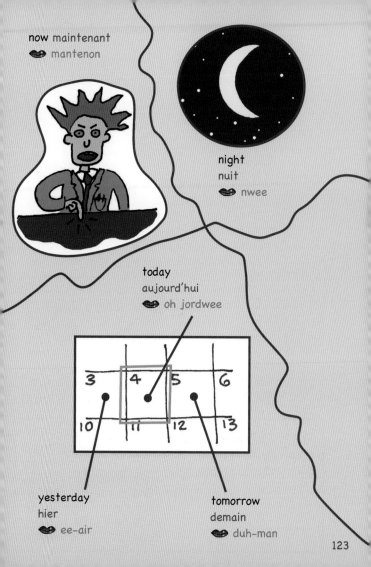

now maintenant
🗣 mantenon

night
nuit
🗣 nwee

today
aujourd'hui
🗣 oh jordwee

yesterday
hier
🗣 ee-air

tomorrow
demain
🗣 duh-man

123

# Weather wise

Can we go out?
On peut sortir?
 on puh sorteer

It's hot
Il fait chaud
 eel fay show

It's cold
Il fait froid
 eel fay frwa

It's horrible
Il fait mauvais
 eel fay movay

## It's raining ropes!

In French it doesn't rain "cats and dogs", it rains "ropes"! That's what they say when it's raining really heavily: Il pleut des cordes *(eel pluh day kord)*.

It's windy
Il fait du vent
🗨 eel fay dew von

It's sunny
Il fait du soleil
🗨 eel fay dew solay

It's raining
Il pleut
🗨 eel pluh

It's snowing
Il neige
🗨 eel nej

I'm soaked
Je me suis fait tremper
🗨 juh muswee fay trompay

It's nice Il fait beau
🗨 eel fay bow

125

## Signs of life

Taille Minimum

Minimum Height

Eteindre les téléphones

Turn off your phone

Entrée Interdite

No Entry

Interdit aux moins de dix-huit ans

Under 18s not allowed

Jusqu'à 5 ans
Under 5s only

PRIVATE

PRIVÉ

Messieurs

Dames

Cheat sheet

No Non 🫦 non

Yes Oui 🫦 wee

Hi! Salut! 🫦 saloo

Thanks
Merci 🫦 mer-see

Where?
Où?
🫦 oo

How much?
Combien? 🫦 kombee-yah

Please (to grown-ups)
S'il vous plaît
🫦 seel voo play

(to children) S'il te plaît
🫦 seel tuh play

Bye! au revoir 🫦 oh rev-wa